DERBY CATH

ਸਤਿ ਸ੍ਰੀ ਅਕਾਲ   Benvenuto

Bienvenue

Добро пожаловать   السلام علیکم   W

नमस्ते   Welcome   欢迎光临

FROM THE DEAN

Welcome to the Cathedral Church of All Saints, Derby! The glass doors invite you to come inside. What a surprise awaits you when you enter. A jewel of a building, glittering with life and colour, especially when the sun shines in through the plain glass windows. Despite all the fascinating monuments around the walls, and an unfolding history of a thousand years, your eye is nevertheless drawn immediately to the altar, reminding you that here is, above all else, a place of prayer and worship, a house where people may find God.

We are glad you have come. We hope your visit will be a blessing to you. We pray each day for our visitors and invite you to pray for us. We invite you to return. May God bless you.

A detail of the gilded and painted wrought iron gates that greet the Cathedral visitor, made by Robert Bakewell c.1730.

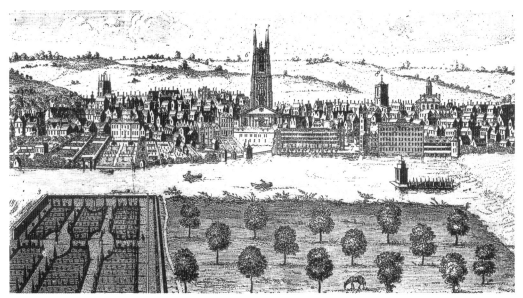

Opposite: Irongate, Derby c.1865, by Louise Rayner
Courtesy of Derby Museum and Art Gallery

Derby in 1728

THE HISTORY OF ALL SAINTS, DERBY

In the late nineteenth and early twentieth centuries, the rapid increase in the population of the country resulted in the creation of new dioceses, and – apart from a few instances where new cathedrals were built (for example Truro and Liverpool) – existing parish churches were chosen to become the seats of the new bishops. The Cathedral Church of All Saints, hallowed in 1927, is one of these.

Thus, the history of All Saints is also that of a parish church – one on a site on which worship has been offered to God in the name of Jesus Christ for over a thousand years.

It was probably founded by King Edmund in 943 as a royal collegiate church with a Dean and six prebendaries, or canons. Early in the twelfth century, King Henry I made a gift of the church to Lincoln Cathedral, whose Dean thus became also the Dean of All Saints. He appointed a Sub-Dean to act in his absence; memorials to two of these still exist. The canons, together with many minor clerics, attendants and domestics lived in buildings along the north side of the church – still known as 'College Place', though the present buildings are eighteenth century.

No visible trace remains of the Saxon Church. At some time during the fourteenth century a new church was built, though whether this replaced the original or a later one is not certain. Indeed not much is known in detail about the medieval building; a ground plan of about 1600 and one or two later drawings show it to have been of about the same size as the present church (without the Retrochoir) with a nave and chancel, a shorter north aisle and a longer south aisle which included St. Katharine's Quire and incorporated a south porch. There was a pinnacled rectangular tower at the west end. This may have been structurally unstable, for it was pulled down and a new tower, in the contemporary Perpendicular style, was built between 1510 and 1530 and still dominates the city today.

From its foundation, All Saints (at various times also called 'All Hallows'), being both 'royal' and 'free', was not answerable to the Bishop of the diocese (then Lichfield and Coventry) and hostility to episcopal authority continued well into the eighteenth century. It is therefore somewhat ironic that in the course of time All Saints should become a Cathedral with its own Bishop.

Before the Reformation the church was richly appointed, with at least six altars, many statues of saints before which candles would be lit, and sumptuous vestments and plate, but in 1549, in the reign of Edward VI, the College was dissolved, the priests turned out and all the rich trappings sold or destroyed. In 1556, during the brief return of the Papal Supremacy, Mary Tudor, perhaps remembering All Saints' royal origins,

granted pensions to the dispossessed canons and allocated the rents of some of the properties previously owned by the College to the Bailiffs and Burgesses of Derby – later the Corporation – to provide two priests for the church. Thus the Corporation became responsible for the upkeep of the Chancel, and the living of the church remained securely outside the jurisdiction of the Bishop. Also in 1556, All Saints acquired its own martyr. She was Joan Waste, a poor blind woman living in the parish and going every day to the church where the clerk would read the New Testament to her. She could not accept the doctrine of transubstantiation and under the re-introduced heresy laws was burned as a heretic at the age of twenty-two.

In 1607 Elizabeth Countess of Shrewsbury - better known as **BESS OF HARDWICK** *- was buried in the vault below St. Katharine's Quire in the South aisle of the medieval church. An elaborate monument, designed and built under her prior supervision, was erected above and thus began a long association with the Cavendish family, descendants from her marriage to Sir William Cavendish - the second of her four husbands. By the middle of the nineteenth century, when new arrangements were made at Edensor, some forty four coffins occupied the vaults, including the equally famous Georgiana, Duchess of Devonshire, who was buried here in 1806.*

Courtesy of Hardwick Hall,
The Devonshire Collection.
(The National Trust)/.NTPL

As a 'royal peculiar', the Parish of All Saints was entitled to grant its own marriage licences, probates of wills etc., normally a diocesan prerogative (the privilege was withdrawn in 1857). In 1634, a Consistory Court was built to facilitate these functions and for the holding of bishops' and archdeacons' visitations. This comprised a high canopied seat in a railed enclosure and was set up in St. Katharine's Quire. It may now be seen in the North Aisle.

Derby seems to have escaped the worst excesses of the Civil War and the Puritan era, though the church accounts of the period record above-average glass replacement and also the levelling of the Chancel in 1646. All Saints had a Puritan minister, John Swetnam, from 1643 until he resigned in 1662, in anticipation of the Act of Uniformity following the Restoration. From the middle of the seventeenth century the fabric of the church appears to have deteriorated steadily and by the end of it the general condition could be described as ruinous. In February 1723 the Vicar, Dr. Michael Hutchinson, arbitrarily began its demolition over-night. The Corporation, which until then had been dilatory in its responsibilities regarding the Chancel, accepted the *fait accompli* and headed the subscription list for a new church.

Hutchinson chose as architect James Gibbs, who had recently designed St. Mary-le-Strand and St. Martin-in-the Fields in London. The builder was Francis Smith of Warwick. Gibbs' church, a simple rectangular building in the classical style and married to the retained sixteenth century tower and porch, extended as far as the present position of the high altar, with a large three-light Venetian east window. To alleviate the somewhat severe interior, he included in his design a wrought-iron screen extending across the whole width of the church. A local iron-smith and gate-maker, Robert Bakewell, was commissioned to make the screen, which was finished some five years after the first sermon was preached in the new church on 25th November 1725.

JAMES GIBBS, *the architect of the present Cathedral with a representation of the Church in 1827.*

The raising of the necessary funds to pay for the new church was a constant problem which may have unhinged Dr Hutchinson's mind, for he found himself in a series of disputes culminating in his resignation in 1728. He died eighteen months later, leaving the accounts in confusion and many debts outstanding. Despite all these difficulties, the new church soon became popular with the citizens of Derby. Though many of the old memorials were lost, some of the best were re-installed - including that of Bess of Hardwick.

The Earl of Exeter, who at that time had a house in Full Street near the eastern end of the church, gave a splendid set of SILVER-GILT PLATE, *as well as various furnishings.*

The old Consistory Court was placed in the North Aisle, embellished with a Bakewell candlestick and a carved inscription, and used for Corporation as well as ecclesiastical business.

In December 1745, the church received a royal and historic visitor, HRH PRInCE CHARLES EDWARD STUART *- the 'Young Pretender'. His army had marched almost unhindered from Carlisle, and camped around the town to rest before pressing on to London.*

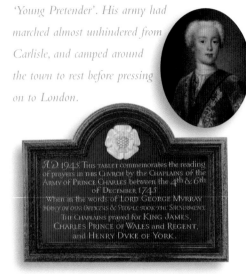

Tablet commemorating the bicentenary of the visit of the Young Pretender - "Bonnie Prince Charlie". It is on the south wall near the steps to St. Katharine's Chapel.

The Young Pretender is known to have ordered the bells of All Saints to be rung and to have attended with his officers a service held in the church - though the form this took is not reliably recorded. At a council held on the following day the Prince was persuaded by his staff to abandon the march to London. He retreated to Scotland and to ultimate defeat at Culloden. It is interesting to speculate on the course political and ecclesiastical history might have taken had the decision taken that day in Derby been to march on!

Few major changes were made to the fabric of the church during the two hundred years following the completion of Gibbs' work.

The side galleries at the west end were added in 1841 to cope with the increasing population, extending the small musicians' gallery provided by Gibbs in 1733. The nineteenth century passion for the 'beautification' of churches resulted in the loss of some of Bakewell's ironwork both inside and outside; Gibbs' box pews were replaced by the bench type still in use and the clear windows were filled with patterned coloured glass. In 1894 the choir was moved from the organ gallery to the Chancel, and new carved oak choir stalls designed by Temple Moore (who had earlier produced a new pulpit) were installed.

However, the most significant event of this period was the creation of the new diocese of Southwell in 1884 and the transfer of practically the whole of the County of Derbyshire from the See of Lichfield to the new see, which also included much of Nottinghamshire, hived off from the diocese of Lincoln. In 1889 the first suffragan, or assistant, bishop to the diocesan Bishop of Southwell was appointed, with the title of Bishop of Derby. He and his successor worked hard with the first Bishops of Southwell for the creation of a new diocese of Derby and this was brought to fruition with the hallowing of All Saints as its Cathedral Church on 28th October, 1927, the first Bishop being enthroned on the following day.

The Cathedral from the south west in the mid-19th century.

Sebastian
COMPER
F.R.I.B.A.
1891 ✝ 1979

*Architect of
the extension to
this Cathedral*

*Above: The east end of the Cathedral showing
Sebastian Comper's extension, with a graphic
detail of the wall tablet commemorating his life.*

From the start it had been appreciated that the church, although large by parish standards, was too small for the great diocesan occasions; it was not however until 1965 that work could be started on the eastern extension. The architect was Sebastian Comper, modifying the earlier and somewhat grander designs of his father, Sir Ninian Comper. The work was completed early in 1972 and provided a

Retrochoir with Chapter Room beneath, flanked by a Sacristy, Song School and various offices. The great baldachin (or baldacchino) over the high altar was introduced at this time.

St. Katharine's Chapel, south of the Chancel, was dismantled during the Comper re-ordering to allow a processional route from the Song School. In 1978 the outer part of the Cavendish burial vault was converted into a small Crypt Chapel retaining the old dedication to St. Katharine, for occasional services, private prayer and reservation of the Blessed Sacrament.

Just outside the screen in the south aisle are the steps leading down to the Chapel. The altar here is of polished Derbyshire crinoidal limestone (340 million years old), containing a myriad fossils of small sea creatures. The bronze crucifix on the wall is by a Derbyshire sculptor, Ronald Pope. It is used also as a Lenten processional cross.

*St. Katharine's
Chapel with the
crucifix by
Ronald Pope.*

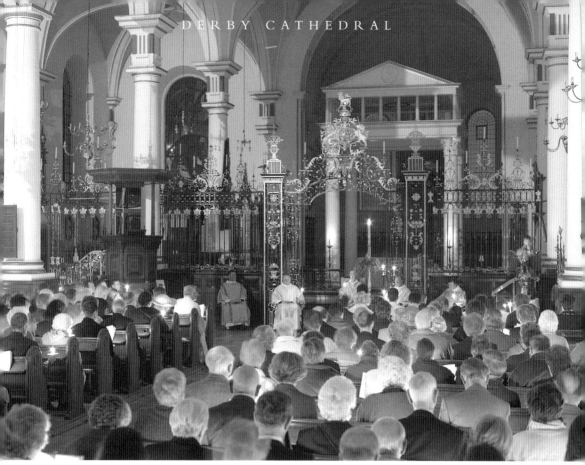

The Easter Liturgy late on Easter Eve.

Thanksgiving Service for the Queen's Golden Jubilee, June 2002.

Courtesy of Derby Evening Telegraph

Photograph ~ W.H. Marks

A Living Church

Like all other cathedrals, Derby is much more than a beautiful building. It is, as its constitution states, 'the seat of the Bishop and a centre of worship and mission'. The Bishop gathers the clergy and people of the Diocese of Derby here for the ordinations of new priests and deacons, for the baptism of new Christians and for confirmation, for the blessing of the holy oils on Maundy Thursday and for other great diocesan occasions. Additionally he presides at the liturgy in the Cathedral at Christmas, Easter and other principal festivals.

The Cathedral is governed by the Dean and the Chapter - four priests, known as canons, and four lay people. The Dean and Canons have a particular responsibility for maintaining the daily worship of the Cathedral, as well as managing its life and ministry, assisted by the lay staff and many volunteers. Its mission involves schools work and adult education, welcome and hospitality to visitors, pilgrims and to people in distress of one kind or another, sharing the Christian faith and engaging in dialogue with enquirers and with those of other faiths, and working in close co-operation with the City, the University and other institutions.

Each day the Eucharist, with its origins in the Last Supper on the night before Jesus died, is celebrated around the altar in the Cathedral. On Sundays and festivals it is a sung service, with one of the Cathedral's three choirs leading the music and with the participation of the Cathedral's regular congregation, which also contributes much to its life through the week. The Cathedral also hosts many occasions through the year when the wider communities of city and county come to mark significant occasions in local and national life. It is the setting also for concerts, recitals, festivals and exhibitions.

Amidst all this activity in what is very much a 'working cathedral', there are nevertheless long periods of calm and quiet and visitors are always welcome to walk round, to sit and enjoy its peace, to join in worship, to light a candle or to pray.

Photograph: Anne Johns

The Tower

The late Perpendicular tower is built in Ashover grit from Duffield Bank quarry. Fifty feet square at the base, it rises to a height of 212 feet to the top of the pinnacles.

Painting by Roy Berry of the Cathedral from Queen Street, hanging in the Sacristy.

Various dates have been given for its construction but from the first volume of the Churchwardens' minute books it appears that work was in progress in the second year of Henry VIII's reign in 1511, and it may not have been finished before 1532, in which year Church Ales were held in Chaddesden, Brailsford and Wirksworth to raise funds for the completion. 'Ales' were a popular means of raising money for church expenses, against which the bazaars and car-boot sales of the present day seem uninspired. Special ale was brewed and cakes baked and the feasting was accompanied by morris dancing, the presentation of mystery plays, and sports. The accounts of the time record generous benefactions and also the payments to the master mason, John Otes, who had previously worked on King's College at Cambridge. The view of the south elevation from the churchyard typifies the three periods of the present building. Sebastian Comper's new east end, built in reconstituted stone, is weathering to harmonise with the south wall of Gibbs' church, with its six great windows framed in Coxbench stone and topped by its impressive balustrade.

The words 'Young Men and Maidens' (Psalm 148), carved along the string course of the south face is thought to indicate that the young people of the town paid for the first stage of building. The same words appear on the north side but in an older script and not so legibly.

The Bells

The bell chamber at the top of the tower contains a fine ring of ten bells, all over 300 years old, and a carillon plays various tunes on the bells three times each weekday.

The earliest records imply that there were five bells at All Saints as long ago as 1509. However, apart from the possible exception of the tenor, it is certain that these bells were replaced or recast in the next hundred years or so. In 1620 the five bells were augmented to six by the addition of a treble - the present fifth bell in the ring of ten. This bell was cast by George Oldfield of Nottingham and bears the inscription 'Batchelers Bell'. The history behind the inscription is most interesting. It appears that a company in the town started a lottery and several young men of the parish 'subscribed three guineas to be adventured in it'. Their enterprise was rewarded and they won £12, which they donated towards the cost of the new treble. Until 1926, when the bells were retuned and rehung on an iron frame, the 'Batchelers Bell' was a maiden bell, that is, it was not in

need of tuning when taken from the mould after casting.

The heaviest bell of the original six, and the present tenor, is the oldest bell in the tower and is well over 500 years old. The other four - the present sixth, seventh, eighth and ninth - were also cast by the Oldfields at dates between 1607 and 1655. Little is known of how or why these bells were acquired by the Cathedral, but they probably replaced the older bells.

In 1677 the ring of six was augmented to ten by William Noone of Nottingham by the addition of four trebles. Thus we see that the present ten bells, apart from a relatively recent refugee from Ashbourne, have been at Derby Cathedral for over 300 years. None of the bells has been recast and, considering this, the bells are of surprisingly good tone.

The bells were rehung on a wooden frame in 1687 and again, on the present iron frame, when All Saints' became a Cathedral in 1927.

The entrance gates between the street and the West door came from a now demolished house in St. Mary's Gate opposite. They date from the early 18th century and were made by Robert Bakewell and replace those made by him for the Cathedral but inexplicably sold off during road widening in the 1870s.

The west window in the porch shows four heraldic shields surmounted by episcopal mitres. The first has the arms of the Province of Canterbury, of which the Diocese of Derby is a part. The second has those of the Diocese of Lichfield, in which Derby lay until 1884, and the third those of Southwell, to which it was transferred in that year. The fourth shows the arms of the new see of Derby which combine St. Chad's distinctive Cross of Lichfield and the three fountains, or wells, of Southwell.

At the front of the centre aisle are the two civic pews. That on the south side is the *Mayor's pew* and is decorated with Bakewell ironwork incorporating a painted representation of the City badge - a stag enclosed by palings, colloquially known as the Buck in the Park. There are stands for the civic sword and maces.

Above the doors leading into the Nave is the central gallery, accommodating the totally-enclosed *Compton organ* with its 3,077 pipes, including over 1,500 from the preceding instruments of 1808 and 1879. It was built in 1939, but did not acquire its impressive case, designed by Sebastian Comper, until 1963. It is played from a four-manual console in the Consistory Court area. The galleries on either side of the organ - not included in Gibbs' design - were added in 1841. Beyond the galleries, the spaciousness and light of the interior can be appreciated. The arcading of the nave and chancel is carried on stone Roman columns with Doric capitals. The panelling round the bases of the columns indicates the height of the original box pews, which were replaced by the present benches in 1873.

On the north side is the *County Council pew.* This was established in 1972 and is fitted with iron-work to the design of the then Cathedral architect, Anthony New, symbolising the topography, resources and industry of the county.

Across the whole width of the nave and aisles is the magnificent *wrought-iron screen*, designed by Gibbs to alleviate the somewhat severe simplicity of his nave, and made by the Derby smith, Robert Bakewell (1682-1752), whose work may be found over much of the Midlands and beyond. Aptly described as 'delicate as lace and intricate as a fugue', it separates nave and chancel without obscuring the view. Bakewell was paid for the screen in 1730, its assumed completion date; subsequent re-siting and even removal to suit changes in liturgical fashions resulted in much damage and loss, but the central parts are substantially original and the remainder faithfully restored. The overthrow over the central gates carries the Royal Arms, placed here, as in other forms in countless Parish churches throughout the country, to signify the Monarch's position in the Church of England. The arms are of interest, being those of George II and including the fleur-de-lys of France in the top right quarter and below that the arms of the House of Hanover.

The parclose screens on either side of the Chancel are modern, but the small gate on the north side is original Bakewell. It came from a private house in the town. The overthrow, being beyond repair, has been replaced by modern work incorporating the pilgrims' scallop shells and having a pelican, widely used as a Christian symbol, for the crest.

The pulpit

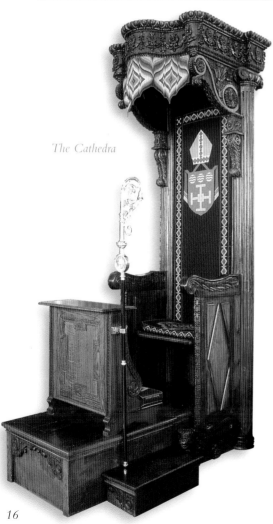

The Cathedra

A detail of the intricately carved pulpit

The pulpit and

Chancel stalls are by Temple Moore, dating from 1873 and 1894 respectively. The stalls, originally for the choir, have been re-ordered to accommodate the members of the College of Canons.

Here the Dean and Canons gather at the heart of a community that prays here every day - saying or singing Morning or Evening prayer, very often with one of the Cathedral choirs.

The *Bishop's throne,* or *Cathedra,* is on the north side of the

Chancel. The Cathedra is Greek Orthodox in origin. The upper part is believed to have been an icon stand of the 16th century, the seat being added in the 17th. It was found in Constantinople. The canvas-work Florentine decoration of the throne and the cushions in the stalls were made by members of the Cathedral's own embroidery workshop, as were the banners flanking the altar. One of these depicts the symbols of All Saints - the crown and scrolls inscribed 'Sanctus, Sanctus, Sanctus', the other the Seal of the old Collegiate Church. The original seal, dating from the 14th century, is still in the possession of the Cathedral.

The baldachin, or canopy, over the High Altar forms part of Sebastian Comper's design for the eastern extension of the Cathedral. Its angular pediment and Corinthian columns contrast dramatically with the interacting curves of Gibbs' nave ceiling and the simplicity of his Roman Doric pillars and capitals. The golden ceiling of the baldachin itself is part of the tester designed by Ninian Comper (father of Sebastian) which was suspended over the altar from 1927. It incorporates the representation of the Holy Spirit in the form of a dove with the seven gifts of the Spirit radiating from it.

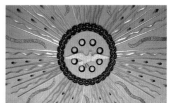

DERBY CATHEDRAL

On the east wall of the Retrochoir is a small *two-manual organ*, which is mainly used to accompany the Choir. It is decorated with *cherubs' heads* which are all that is left of the 18th century west-end organ case. The Retrochoir also contains a fine *three-seat sedilia* in carved oak, a memorial to Edmund Pearce, the first diocesan Bishop of Derby.

At the east end of the north and south aisles are the only two *coloured windows.* These were installed in 1965 and are the work of Ceri Richards, the distinguished Welsh artist

who died in 1971. Their sharp clear blues and yellows, their fluent abstract shapes and patterns, are more basic and elemental than anything else in the Cathedral. They are like glimpses of a primordial struggle between darkness and light. In fact that is what they are, except that the serene harmonies of the right hand window express the ultimate triumph of light. The artist designed them round the two traditional concepts of All Souls and All Saints, in reference to the Cathedral's dedication, and the conflict implied in the All Souls window (on the left) represents the human soul emerging from its physical limitations, while the All Saints window depicts its consummation.

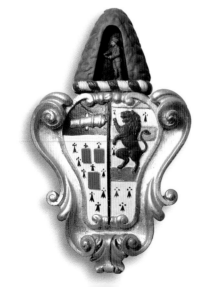

On the North wall, adjacent to the All Souls' window is a *fine monument* to the Chambers family, by Louis Roubiliac, with iron railings attributed to Bakewell. The crest of the coat of arms deserves inspection. It shows a miner at work, an acknowledgement of the source of the family wealth.

18

Also in this area is the *Consistory Court.* This canopied wooden structure was set up in 1643 and re-instated in the new church in 1725. Note the carved inscription on the chair back and the iron candlestick added by Bakewell. This Court was used for the hearing of ecclesiastical legal matters, usually with the Archdeacon 'in the chair'; municipal legalities would also be heard.

Next to the Court is the *alabaster memorial slab to John Lawe*, one of the Sub-deans of the old Collegiate Church. This, now upright, was originally a floor slab and, much restored, shows him in 15th century vestments and holding a chalice. Oddly, the date of his death was never cut in the space provided for it. He is known to have been alive in 1440.

On the other side of the Chancel is the Cavendish Area, where several of the Cathedral's treasures are found. This statue of the *Blessed Virgin Mary and Child* formerly stood in the Convent Chapel of the Community of the Holy Name at Malvern Link. It was given into the care of the Cathedral in 1990 when the Community moved to Oakwood in the County and Diocese of Derby.

Joseph Wright of Derby's

tombstone, which was in St. Werburgh's churchyard, was brought into the Cathedral in the year 2002. It is known to be an 18th century re-use of a medieval vault marker.

Joseph Wright (1734 - 1797) was an important artist who lived and worked in Derby. He is recognised internationally today as a major figure of his time and Derby Museum and Art Gallery holds the best collection of his work. Beginning as a portrait painter for noteworthy patrons such as Sir Richard Arkwright, his range and interests developed, and today his pictures are recognised for their spectacular use of light and shadow, evoking the theatrical moods of nature, and often display Wright's excitement and fascination for scientific discovery and industrial invention.

Early self portrait, c. 1753, when Wright was about 20.

A Philosopher lecturing on the Orrery (1766)

Arguably Wright's most famous painting, this holds an interesting connection with the Cathedral. The lecturer is reputedly a portrait of Charles Denby, organist at All Saints and author of some musical pieces now in Derby Local Studies Library. Wright played the flute at musical evenings at Denby's house. The man taking notes is undoubtedly Peter Burdett, map-maker, who played the cello at the same musical evenings.

Pictures courtesy of Derby Museum and Art Gallery

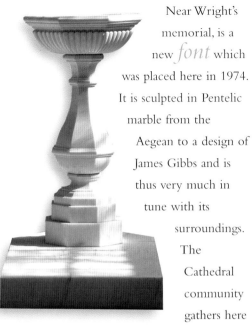

Near Wright's memorial, is a new *font* which was placed here in 1974. It is sculpted in Pentelic marble from the Aegean to a design of James Gibbs and is thus very much in tune with its surroundings. The Cathedral community gathers here whenever a Baptism is celebrated.

means the sun could represent the constellation Leo, since the face is lion-like. It is intriguing to ponder the possible origins of the plank. It could have been part of a representation of the Last Judgement (paintings of which were commonly found in Courts of justice) adorning the Consistory Court, which was originally erected in 1635. Other views on its source suggest a fragment of the top of a reredos panel representing Our Lord in Glory or The Creation. Others feel it is part of a non-Christian picture which may have had a secular use.

The plank was rehung in its present position in 1997, thanks to financial support from The Friends of Derby Cathedral.

The Derby Plank

When Cathedral repairs were carried out in 1948, this plank was found, having a painted scene on the underside. Restoration by Anna Hulbert in 1997 revealed details of the picture and clues to its possible age.
The starry sky with a moon and the expression on the face of the sun suggest that it could possibly belong to the late 16th or early 17th century. The six painted stars are Gothic in character and the unruffled clouds are similar to those on a painted ceiling in Staunton Harold church in Leicestershire, which dates from 1655.
The sun's rays end abruptly at the top of the board. Might there have been another plank above this? The rainbow looks as if it has always been at the bottom edge of the composition. The presence of a night sky

This part of the church is on the site of the medieval St. Katharine's Quire and contains the flamboyant monument of *Bess of Hardwick* (1518 - 1607). Bess had this designed by Smithson (architect of Bolsover Castle) and made before her death so that she should be worthily remembered. She is interred in the vault below, together with many of her Cavendish descendants. The

beautifully engraved coffin plates of some of these are affixed to the panelling. They include that of Henry Cavendish, the renowned scientist who first isolated hydrogen and also - remarkably accurately - calculated the weight of the Earth.

Here also are two fine monuments, one of *Caroline Countess of Bessborough* daughter of the 3rd Duke of Devonshire, which is by Rysbrack, and one of William Ponsonby, Earl of Bessborough, by Nollekens.

West of the Bakewell screen is found another Sub-dean's memorial. This is unusual, being made of wood (at one time it was apparently painted to represent stone!). It possibly represents *Robert Johnson*, known to be *Sub-dean* in 1527 and therefore one of the last before the Dissolution. It was banished to the crypt in 1723 and forgotten until the late 19th century by which time it needed extensive restoration. The carving beneath, believed to represent the 13 Bedesmen who received grants to pray for his soul, was retained in the new church and escaped damage. Below this is an example of the curious custom of including a representation of a shrouded corpse to remind beholders of the humble reality behind the pomp of the memorial.

The Chapel of St. Mary on the Bridge

Within walking distance of the Cathedral is an unsung treasure of Derby. One of the very few surviving bridge chapels in England, it still continues to be used as a place of worship. This beautiful and fascinating building dates from the 14th century and houses many architectural clues to the Chapel's intriguing and varied history.

Although a separate building, it serves as a chapel of the Cathedral, as well as having a regular congregation of its own.

ALL SAINTS' PARISH REGISTERS

These date from 1558, though it had been decreed in 1538 that records should be kept of all baptisms, marriages and burials in every parish, and in fact the entries up to 1598 are copied from the first register, now lost. Until 1610 All Saints' register was in Latin, when the Minister, one Richard Kilby, decided that this was old-fashioned and wrote 'I see no reason why a register for English people should be written in Latin' at the top of a page: thereafter, English became the rule.

After 1754 separate books had to be used for burials, baptisms and marriages, and by the end of the 18th century, books containing printed forms, requiring only to be filled in with names and dates, were used. This, while tidier, meant that there was now no room for the interesting and often entertaining notes about contemporary events, and details about individuals, which had found their way into the registers. The following are a few examples of entries of this type:

On the flyleaf of the earliest book – 'A poor blind woman called Joan Waste of this parish, a martyr, burned in Windmill Pit, 1st. of August 1556'.

1593 – a comment on the enormous number of burials of those who died 'ex Peste' (of the Plague) – 'It ceased upon a sudden at what time it was dispersed in every corner of this whole parish, there was not two houses together free from it'.

1610 – 'Buried William Norman who was drowned, God knoweth how. O God be merciful unto us sinners that we may fear thee and always be prepared to die well. Amen'.

1642-3 – Several local incidents of the Civil War are recorded, such as the siege of Lichfield.

January 1649 – 'King Charles I was beheaded at Whitehall the 30th day'.

1774 – 'Buried Mary, widow of William Vickers – inhumanly murdered in her own house' and the sequel 'For this murder Mathew Cocklayne was apprehended in Ireland and executed here March 1776 and hung in irons in Bradshaw Hay' – a tribute to 18th century detective methods.

In the 18th century the custom grew of inserting the age of those buried. Well over half of these are children, with smallpox often mentioned as the cause of death.

We hope you have found here a holy place of hospitality, a centre of worship and of mission, welcoming all people of goodwill today. We pray that the grace and mercy of God our Father and the Lord Jesus Christ may go with you.

Detail of the Cathedral's best new vestments, designed and made by Leonard Childs in the Cathedral workshop, and reflecting the pattern on the sarcophagus of St. Alkmund, Patron Saint of the City, to be found in the Derby Museum and Art Gallery.